THE NOTEBOOK OF DOOM

POP OF THE BUMPY MUMMY

by Troy Cummings

BRANCHES™
SCHOLASTIC INC.

TABLE OF CONTENTS

To Bailey: When are we going to play some more board games? How about a week from Saturday? 8:30 sound good? Great—see you then!

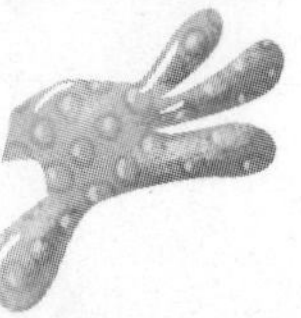

Thank you, Katie Carella and Liz Herzog, for making my work pop!

Library of Congress Cataloging-in-Publication Data

Cummings, Troy, author.
Pop of the bumpy mummy / by Troy Cummings.
pages cm. - (The Notebook of Doom ; 6.)
Summary: Alexander's class is going on a sleepover at the Stermont Museum, but something is stealing bright, shiny objects from all over town, including the museum's treasured Ruby Scorpion, and on the night of the visit the young monster hunters finally confront the town's newest monster-a warrior covered entirely by bubble-wrap.
ISBN 0-545-69898-6 (pbk. : alk. paper) - ISBN 0-545-69899-3 (jlb : alk. paper) - ISBN 0-545-69901-3 (ebook)
1. Monsters-Juvenile fiction. 2. Elementary schools-Juvenile fiction. 3. Museums-Juvenile fiction. 4. Horror tales.
[1. Monsters-Fiction. 2. Elementary schools-Fiction. 3. Schools-Fiction. 4. Museums-Fiction. 5. Horror stories.] I. Title.
II. Series: Cummings, Troy. Notebook of doom ; 6.

PZ7.C91494Pop 2015
813.6-dc23

ISBN- 13: 978-93-5103-819-1

Book design by Liz Herzog

First Scholastic printing, January 2015

This edition September 2019

Printed at Shivam Offset Press, New Delhi

CHAPTER 1 JUNK MAIL

Alexander Bopp was almost home when he heard the screaming. It was coming from his house.

He ran to his yard. His dad was on the front porch, twisting and shouting.

"Dad?!" he yelled.

Alexander had seen lots of weird things since moving to Stermont. Weird things like *monsters*. He'd battled balloon goons, shadow smashers, tunnel fish, and other creepy creatures.

Alexander looked from the porch to the trees to the driveway. No monsters. *Oh, wait — Dad's not under attack,* he thought. *He's dancing!*

"Good news, Al!" his dad said. "It's finally here!"

Alexander's dad boogied into the house. Alexander followed, dropping his backpack by the door. "*What's* here, Dad?"

His dad spun around, holding a padded envelope. "The Reflecto-900 is here!" he said. He ripped open the envelope and pulled out a golden wand. "It's the perfect dental tool!"

Alexander gave his dad a funny look.

"Geez, Al!" his dad said. "If you were a dentist, you'd be going *nuts* about this mirror!" He polished the Reflecto-900 on his sleeve. "Let's see if *your* package is any better."

"*I* have a package?" asked Alexander.

"You sure do," his dad said. "Although it doesn't say who it's from."

He handed Alexander a rainbow-striped box.

It was large, but very light.

"It looks like a birthday present!" said Alexander's dad.

"It can't be," said Alexander. "My birthday isn't until February twenty-ninth. That's months away."

He tore into the box.

"Look at all that bubble wrap!" his dad said. "Whatever is in there *must* be good!"

Alexander dug around in the box. He yanked out a huge blob of bubble wrap.

"It's empty," he said.

"Check again," his dad said. "You must have missed something."

Alexander checked. "Nope," he said. "Just a bunch of bubble wrap." His shoulders slumped.

"Sorry, kiddo," his dad said.

Alexander tossed the box aside. *Why would someone send me an empty box?*

"Tell you what," said Alexander's dad. "Let's have waffles for dinner." He set the Reflecto-900 on the coffee table and walked toward the kitchen.

"Hey, Al," called his dad. "Why don't you bring that box and bubble wrap to school tomorrow — for Packing Day?"

"Oh, yeah — okay," said Alexander, popping a few bubbles.

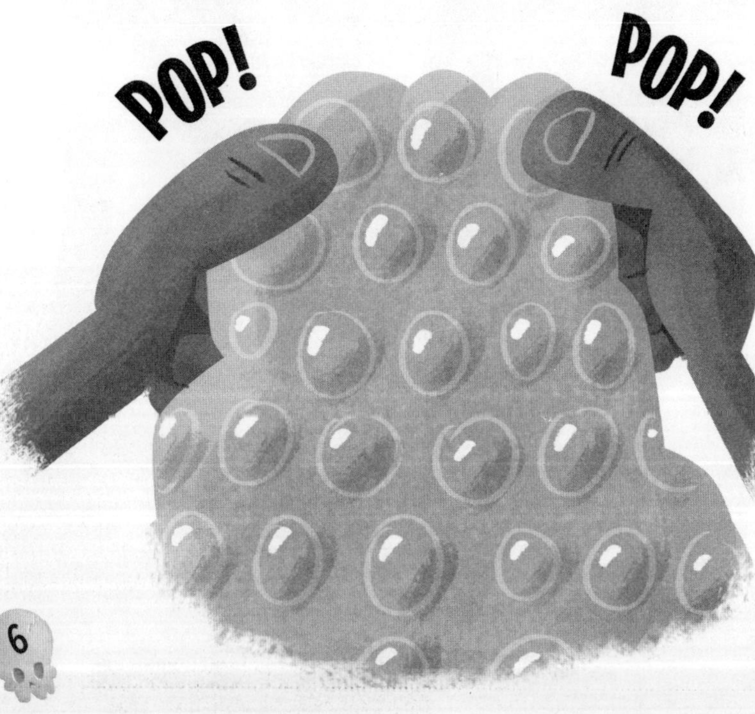

Tomorrow was the last day of school. And Stermont Elementary was getting ready to move into a brand-new building. The principal had asked students to donate boxes.

Alexander looked over at the empty box. Then he dropped the bubble wrap on the coffee table and headed to the kitchen.

CHAPTER

2 PACKING DAY

HONK-HONK-HOONNNNNNNK!!

Alexander knew that honk. It was the old we're-going-to-be-late-for-school-if-you-don't-get-down-here-right-now honk.

"Coming, Dad!" he shouted. He grabbed his box, ran outside, and hopped in the car.

"Did you bring the bubble wrap, too?" asked Alexander's dad.

“No, I couldn’t find it,” said Alexander.

“Well, I’ll be flossed!” said Alexander’s dad. “I can’t find my Reflecto-900, either!”

“You left it on the coffee table last night,” said Alexander.

“I looked there,” said his dad, “but no luck.”

Alexander pulled his spelling book out of his backpack. A piece of paper fell to the seat.

PAJAMA PARTY
at the
STERMONT MUSEUM
Saturday night
sleepover!
CHAPERONES:
* Mr. Plunkett
* Mr. Hoarsely
* Dr. Bopp
See the Ruby Scorpion
and the Bumpy Mummy!
Bring your sleeping bag!
COUPON
10% off any paperweight
at the gift shop!

"Oh, yeah, Dad. The museum sleepover is tomorrow night," said Alexander.

"I know!" his dad grinned. "We're going to have a blast!"

Alexander opened the spelling book. He had tucked an old notebook inside.

The notebook belonged to the Super Secret Monster Patrol. It was their job to keep Stermont safe from monsters. Alexander was one of the club's three members.

He flipped the notebook open.

PURPLE SLURPER

Two arms. Two legs. 39 tongues.

HABITAT Under the dinner table.

~~PETER-PICKER-PIPED-A-PECK~~...

~~PEEPER-PIPER-PECKED-A-PEEP~~...

~~PICKLE-PETER-PEPPED-A~~

These guys hate tongue twisters.

DIET Purple slurpers love to lick chocolate icing and melted popsicles off of people's faces.

BEHAVIOR

Drooling
Slobbering
Stamp-collecting

WARNING! Scrub your face at least once a week, or you might get licked!

"We're here!" said his dad.

Alexander closed the notebook as his dad pulled into the school parking lot. The car stopped beside a sign.

Students and teachers were busy loading boxes into a moving truck.

"Happy Packing Day, Al!" said his dad. "See you after school."

"Thanks, Dad!" said Alexander. He hopped out of the car with his big striped box and — **PLONK!** — walked into someone carrying another big striped box.

"Salamander?" she said.

Salamander was Alexander's nickname. His two friends in the S.S.M.P. called him that. And he had just crashed into one of them.

"Hi, Nikki!" he said. "Hey! Your box looks just like mine!"

"Did yours come in the mail yesterday, too?" she asked.

"Yes!" said Alexander. "But mine was empty. Except for some bubble wrap."

"Same here!" said Nikki.

Suddenly, they heard an angry growl. A wall of cardboard boxes started shaking. Then — **KA-BASH!** It came crashing down.

"Ha! Scared you, weenies!" said a spiky-haired kid. It was Rip Bonkowski, the third, and loudest, member of the S.S.M.P.

"Uh, good one, Rip," Alexander said.

"Hey, look!" said Rip. "Our boxes are triplets!" He held up another striped box.

"Weird . . ." said Alexander. "Three matching boxes?"

"More than three," said Nikki. She pointed to a sign that said BOX DROP-OFF. Students were lined up, all carrying striped boxes.

Alexander counted. "Thirteen . . . fourteen . . . fifteen . . . sixteen matching boxes?!" he said. "That's super strange!"

"Yeah, yeah — *soooo* spooky," said Rip, rolling his eyes. "Let's dump our boxes and get to class."

CHAPTER 3

LAST CLASS

Alexander grabbed the cold, metal handle of the cold, metal door to his cold, metal classroom. Then he paused.

"You guys," he said. "Today is our last day in the morgue!"

"Finally!" said Rip. "Our last day in the room where they used to freeze dead people."

"Next fall, we'll go to an actual *school*," said Nikki, "instead of an old hospital."

Alexander smiled as he yanked open the door one last time.

The room was full of half-packed boxes. In the middle of the boxes sat Mr. Plunkett, a teacher with rainbow suspenders and a bushy mustache.

"Grab a seat, students," said Mr. Plunkett. "If you can find one."

Alexander, Rip, and Nikki sat among the boxes.

Mr. Plunkett stood on a box so he could see everyone. "Our museum sleepover is tomorrow night," he said. "So today's lesson will be about our town's greatest treasure: the Ruby Scorpion!"

Alexander watched his classmates' faces light up.

He raised his hand. “Uh, Mr. Plunkett? What’s a Ruby Scorpion?”

“Oh, right! You’re kind of new to Stermont!” said Mr. Plunkett, hopping down from the box. “I’ve got a super-cool filmstrip about the Ruby Scorpion . . . I’ll just unpack my projector and show you!”

He opened a large, wooden crate.

“Huh?” said Mr. Plunkett. He dug into the crate, tossing aside some bubble wrap. “My projector is gone.”

Mr. Plunkett scratched his mustache.

“Oh, well,” he said. “I’ll draw the Ruby Scorpion for you.”

Mr. Plunkett drew a mean-looking creature on the whiteboard. It had sharp claws and an even sharper tail. "It's a red gem that looks like this," he said.

Nikki raised her hand. "How much is it worth?" she asked.

"Gazillions of dollars!" said Mr. Plunkett.

PIP-PIP-POP!

"Okay, very funny." Mr. Plunkett turned back to the class. "Who's playing with my bubble wrap?"

Alexander looked around. The bubble wrap was nowhere to be seen.

"My projector and the bubble wrap are *both* gone?" said Mr. Plunkett.

He looked at Rip.

"What!?" said Rip. "Why does everyone look at *me* when stuff happens?"

"Well, those things didn't just walk away!" said Mr. Plunkett. He capped his marker. "Fine. Let's move on to math."

Alexander wrote a quick note. He slid it over to Rip and Nikki.

My dad's fancy mirror disappeared this morning—just like Mr. Plunkett's projector . . .

MISSING STUFF + WEIRD STRIPED BOXES = MONSTER?

Rip shook his head as he scribbled on the note. He passed it back.

SALAMANDER = CRAZY x 10!

CHAPTER 4 MUMMY'S THE WORD

A tall, frowning mummy guarded the entrance to the cafeteria. Most students walked right on by. But not Alexander. He stepped up for a closer look.

The mummy was a cardboard cutout. It held the lunch menu.

Alexander skipped the lunch line. He found Rip and Nikki at their usual table. Their plates were piled high with slimy yellow strips.

Rip made gagging sounds. "Do you think the food will be less barfy at our new school?" he asked.

"We can only hope," Nikki said.

BLOOP! BLAP! She dumped a whole jar of salsa on her plate. She mixed it up until her plate was a red, gloppy mess. Then she snarfed it down.

Rip dropped his fork. "You really *do* eat like a monster!" he said.

"Thank you, Rip!" Nikki smiled. She was a monster — a *good* monster called a jampire.

Alexander opened his lunchbox.

Alexander munched an orange slice as he looked back at the fake mummy.

"So, what's the deal with the Bumpy Mummy?" he asked.

"Relax, Salamander," said Rip. "The Bumpy Mummy is just a plain, old museum mummy."

"But it's got these dead, empty eyes," said Nikki. "And it's covered in strange little bumps."

Alexander became covered in strange little bumps. Goose bumps.

"And there's this story," said Nikki, "that the Bumpy Mummy will come alive if someone steals the Ruby Scorpion. But that's —"

"ATTENTION, STUDENTS!"

Alexander jumped. Principal Vanderpants stood behind him, shouting.

"We've already packed our loudspeaker! So I must speak LOUDLY!" she spoke loudly. "Since today is Packing Day, you will spend the rest of the afternoon packing up our school! Report to the loading dock in five minutes!"

Rip groaned.

"No, this is good," said Alexander. "This will give us a chance to learn more about those striped boxes!"

CHAPTER 5 BOXED IN

The loading dock was crowded. Students swarmed around, packing and stacking boxes.

"This place is like a beehive!" said Nikki.

"More like a make-kids-do-all-the-work hive," said Rip.

"Look!" said Nikki. "More striped boxes! They're everywhere!"

"I'm telling you," said Alexander. "These boxes *must* have something to do with monsters!"

"Or the boxes are monsters!" Rip joked.

"Hmmm," said Alexander. "There's only one box monster in the notebook." He flipped it open to show his friends.

YAK-IN-THE-BOX

Dink-a-doo-de-deedle-dee-doo . . .

BOING!! RAARR!! CHOMP!!

HABITAT A polka-dot windup box.

DIET Ladies. Gentlemen. Children of all ages.

SPROING! Yaks-in-the-box get hungry when they hear "Pop Goes the Weasel."

BEHAVIOR This beast may wear a goofy hat, but it does not clown around.

WARNING! Don't turn the crank!

"Our boxes can't be yaks-in-the-box," said Nikki. "Ours are striped."

"If we could just figure out where these boxes came from," said Alexander.

"Let's ask that walking pile of boxes," said Rip.

"Ask me what?" said the walking pile of boxes.

Alexander looked closer. A shock of white hair stuck up from behind the stack of boxes.

"Hey, Mr. Hoarsely!" said Alexander. "What's the deal with these striped boxes?"

Mr. Hoarsely was the school secretary, bus driver, nurse, gym coach, and janitor. He also used to be a member of the S.S.M.P.

"Well, uh . . ." Mr. Hoarsely leaned down. "Someone mailed a box to every kid in Stermont," he said. "And they were all empty, except for —"

P-P-PIP! PIP! POP-POP!

"*Eep!*" Mr. Hoarsely threw his boxes and curled up on the ground. Boxes crashed around him. One landed upside down, covering him like a turtle.

Rip stood nearby, twisting a sheet of bubble wrap. "Oops," he said. "I forgot Hoarsely is such a, uh, scaredy-turtle."

Alexander tapped Mr. Hoarsely's shell. "Did *monsters* send us these boxes?"

Mr. Hoarsely stuck his neck out. "Monsters?! I don't know — and I don't *want* to know!" he said. "I've got my own problems! I had packed Ms. Vanderpants' telescope, but it's missing! And my dustpan is gone, too!" He shuffled off.

"*More* missing stuff?" said Rip. "Maybe you're *not* crazy, Salamander."

"Yeah . . . your dad's mirror, Mr. Plunkett's projector, and now this," said Nikki. "Something is up."

"I agree!" said Alexander, grabbing one of Mr. Hoarsely's boxes. "We've just unpacked a big clue!"

CHAPTER 6 HANDS OFF

The walk home from school was slower than usual.

"Whew!" said Nikki. "I bet we packed twenty thousand things."

"What a lame last day of school," said Rip.

A few minutes later, they stopped in front of Alexander's house.

"All right, guys," said Alexander. "Let's meet at S.S.M.P. headquarters first thing tomorrow. We'll have all day to talk about weird boxes and missing stuff before the sleepover."

"Sounds good!" said Nikki.

"Later," mumbled Rip.

Alexander headed inside — and gasped! The living room had been turned upside down. His dad popped up from behind an overturned armchair. "Hi, Al!" he said.

The room was a jumble of couch cushions, comic books, umbrellas, lamps, and Captain Cuspid action figures.

"I've searched every inch of this room," said Alexander's dad. "The Reflecto-900 is gone!"

KRICKLE!

"What was that?" asked Alexander.

Alexander's dad was rooting around under an end table. "Huh? I didn't hear anything."

KRICKLE-KRICKLE!

Alexander heard the noise again. It sounded like someone crinkling a bag of chips. And it was coming from upstairs! He tiptoed up the steps, listening for the sound.

KRICKLE!

Is someone in our bathroom!? Alexander thought.

He slowly pushed open the door. **CREEEEEAK!**

A wedge of light cut into the dark bathroom.

He stepped inside. The room was silent.

But then — **KRICKLE!** — the shower curtain twitched.

Alexander threw open the shower curtain. Something small and shiny was skittering around the tub like a crab.

A crawling hand! It was grayish-white and crinkly.

"Ack!" Alexander jumped back.

The hand climbed up the shower curtain. It was holding something golden — his dad's mirror!

"Hey!" said Alexander. "Give that back!"

The hand jumped to the windowsill. It used the Reflecto-900 to pry open the window. Then it hopped out.

Alexander rushed to the window. He could see everything in his yard: a tree, his bike, a birdbath. But no crawling hand.

He gasped — someone was behind the tree! A tall, grayish-white, shiny figure. Covered in strange little bumps.

The figure looked up at Alexander. Then it turned and ran down the street.

Alexander's mouth fell open.

The Bumpy Mummy?!

CHAPTER 7 A REAL STEAL

The next morning, Alexander wolfed down his cereal. He was out the door before his spoon hit the table.

He ran through the woods behind his house to an old caboose — the S.S.M.P. headquarters. Rip and Nikki were inside, playing a heated game of tic-tac-tunnel fish.

"You guys," said Alexander, "the Bumpy Mummy is *alive*! I saw it last night!"

Rip and Nikki looked at each other.

Rip snorted. "Come on, Salamander!" he said. "I already told you the Bumpy Mummy is just a bag of bones at the museum."

"No, Rip! I really saw it!" said Alexander. "I mean, I'm pretty sure. It was dark out, and I was kind of far away. But I saw this shiny person, all dressed in white."

"That could have been anyone!" said Rip. "Like a nurse! Or a chef! Or a fencing coach! Not necessarily a monster."

"But it had bumps all over!" said Alexander. "And besides, even if I am wrong about the mummy, I saw something else: a crawling hand! In my bathtub!"

"A monster hand?" said Rip. "Now you're talking!"

"And it had my dad's golden mirror!" said Alexander.

"It did?" Nikki said. "What if that hand monster stole the other missing stuff, too? Like the projector! And the telescope!" She looked at her friends. "It sounds like our new hand monster is a thief!"

"Did you find any hand monsters in the notebook?" asked Rip.

"Yeah," said Alexander. "Sort of."

He opened the monster notebook to a wrinkled-up page.

HITTIN' MITTEN

They look cute, but they pack a punch.

HABITAT Glove compartments.

DIET Lint, fuzz, fur balls.

BEHAVIOR These warm, fuzzy mittens turn into boxing gloves as soon as you put them on. Then: BAM! Stop hitting yourself! Stop hitting yourself!

WARNING! Hittin' mittens work in pairs. If you separate them, they become powerless.

Alexander closed the notebook. "The thing I saw wasn't a mitten — it was a hand . . . with *fingers*," he said.

"All right. Let's spring into action!" said Rip. "So, uh, what should we do?"

"Let's see if anything else is missing," said Alexander. "Go home and snoop around for missing stuff. Then we'll compare notes tonight at the sleepover."

"Sounds like a plan!" said Nikki. "See you on the bus! And watch out for hand monsters!"

The three friends gave one another a high fifteen (high five times three). Then they ran home to start snooping.

CHAPTER

8 'ROUND AND 'ROUND

The sky was as dark as the blacktop in the school parking lot. The only stars out that night were on Alexander's pajama bottoms.

"Nice pants, weenie," said Rip.

"Thanks," said Alexander, giving Rip the stink-eye.

The boys got in line behind Nikki to board the school bus.

"I didn't see *anything* this afternoon," said Alexander. "No crawling hands. No mummies. And no more missing stuff."

"Well," said Rip, "during dinner, my mom said her trumpet had disappeared."

"And my ice skates are missing!" said Nikki.

PSSHHHHT! The bus door opened. Alexander's dad leaned out, waving like a beauty queen.

"Howdy, kiddos!" he said. "I'm Dr. Bopp, Alexander's dad!"

Everyone in line gave Alexander a look. At least, that's how it felt to him.

The students climbed on the bus. Mr. Hoarsely started the engine as Mr. Plunkett took attendance.

Alexander plopped down beside Rip and Nikki.

"Your dad is so cute," said Nikki.

"And his pj's match yours, starpants!" said Rip.

"Yeah, yeah," said Alexander.

The three friends looked out the window as the bus left the parking lot.

"Yikes," said Nikki. "That old hospital is really falling apart."

The bus drove along. It passed a brand-new building.

"Look at our new school!" said Alexander.

"It's so clean and perfect," said Nikki.

"And not smashed up by monsters," said Rip. "At least, not yet."

"It's song time!" Alexander's dad called out from up front. "Here's one I learned at dental school." He took a big breath.

Alexander tried to melt into his seat.

It didn't work.

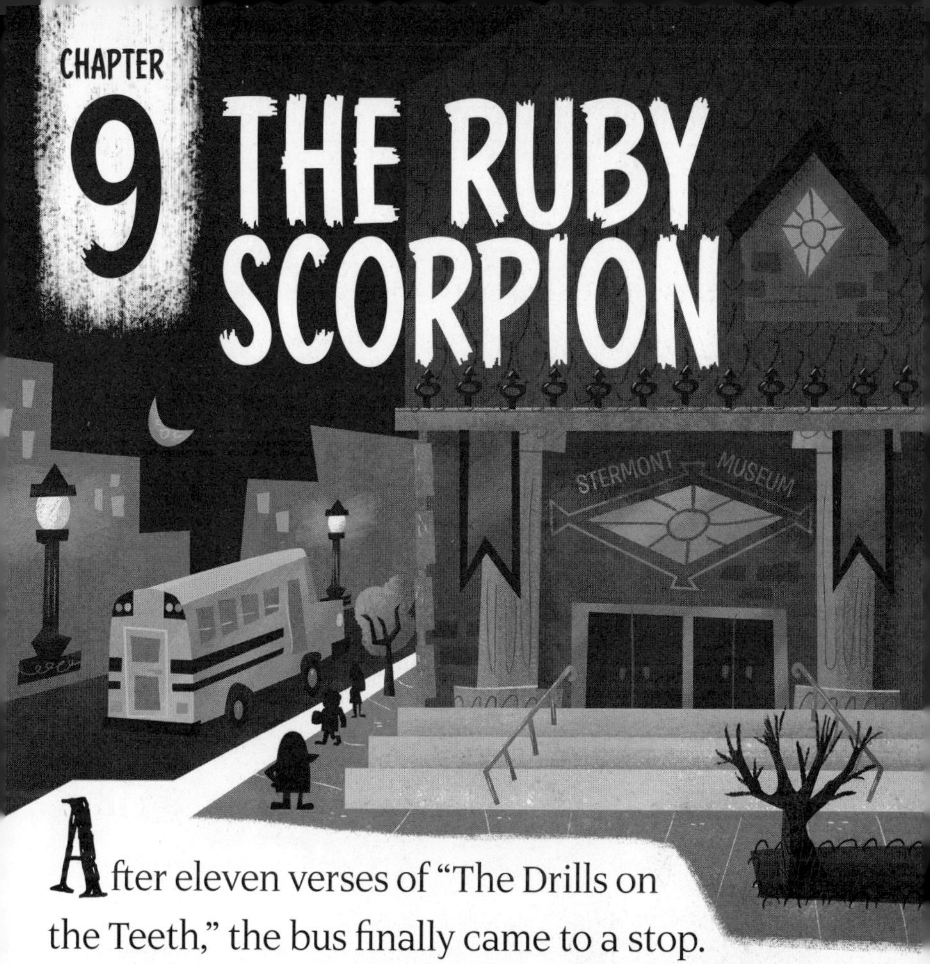

CHAPTER 9 THE RUBY SCORPION

After eleven verses of "The Drills on the Teeth," the bus finally came to a stop.

"We're here!" said Mr. Plunkett. "Grab your gear and head inside."

The Stermont Museum looked like a cross between a bank and a haunted house. Alexander, Rip, and Nikki followed their classmates into the lobby.

The room was big, cold, and dark. A green glow came from an enormous clock on the second floor. Colorful banners hung everywhere.

The BUMPY MUMMY
The RUBY SCORPION
GIFT SHOP

"Okay," said Mr. Plunkett. "Put your sleeping bags over by the gift shop — next to that mean-looking soldier statue."

The statue's head slowly turned to face the group.

Everyone gasped.

"Actually," said the statue, "I am not a statue. I am a guard." She flashed a badge.

Ms. Sargent looked Mr. Plunkett up and down. "My job is to protect Stermont's greatest treasures — and to make sure there's no funny business tonight." She glared at Mr. Plunkett's gopher slippers.

"Funny business?! Me?! Never!" said Mr. Plunkett. "And with Dr. Bopp and Mr. Hoarsely here — wait!" He looked around. "Where *is* Mr. Hoarsely?"

The students stared back in silence.

"Oh, brother," said Mr. Plunkett. "He is always wandering off. Let's just start the tour —"

BONG! CUCKOO!

Mr. Plunkett looked up at the balcony.

"Like I said, let's —"

BONG! CUCKOO!
BONG! CUCKOO!
BONG! CUCKOO!
BONG! CUCKOO!

The students covered their ears.

"What you're hearing is the world's second-largest cuckoo clock," Ms. Sargent said. "It's three stories tall. You'll notice —"

"Clocks schmocks!" yelled Rip. "Let's see the Ruby Scorpion!"

Ms. Sargent gave Rip a look that could wilt lettuce. “Fine,” she said through clenched teeth. “Follow me.”

She led the group to a round room. The room was empty except for a small, glass dome holding the scorpion-shaped red gem. Its eyes seemed to move in the twinkling light.

“Oooooh,” everyone said. They squeezed in for a closer look.

Alexander got separated from Rip and Nikki. *Ugh*, he thought. *The scorpion’s cool and all, but there’s no need to shove.*

"Has anyone ever stolen the Ruby Scorpion?" asked Alexander's dad.

"Impossible!" said Ms. Sargent. "It's protected by my special security system."

She turned off the lights. Thin beams of red light crisscrossed on all sides of the Ruby Scorpion. "To steal the ruby, someone would have to get around all twelve of these lasers. If anything touches a laser, an alarm goes off."

"The ruby . . ." said Mr. Plunkett. "So . . . sparkly."

Everyone stared at the gem in silence.

KRICKLE-KRICKLE!

Alexander's eyes widened. *That's the same crinkling sound I heard last night!*

KRICKLE!

The sound was coming from the lobby. Alexander tried to wave to Rip and Nikki. But like everyone else, they were dazzled by the scorpion.

KRICKLE-KRICKLE!

Alexander backed out of the room. He tiptoed across the lobby.

There!

Something shiny darted across the floor.

A hand! thought Alexander. *The hand from my bathroom!*

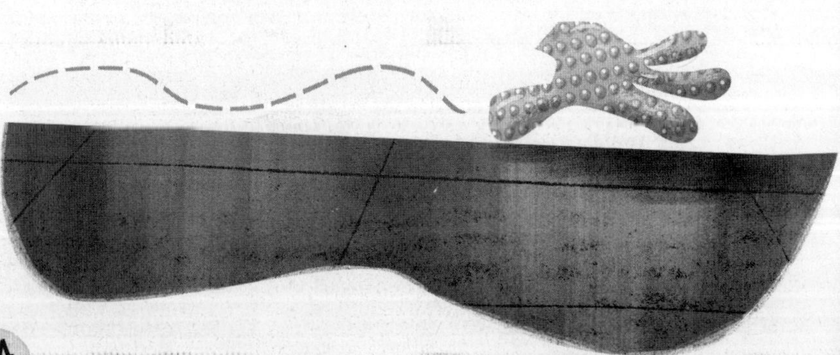

The hand skittered downstairs.

"You're not getting away this time!" Alexander whispered. He dashed down the steps. He skidded to a stop beneath a stone archway.

Alexander swallowed. Then he stepped inside.

CHAPTER 10 JUST IN CASE

Alexander stood in a huge stone room — the mummy's chamber. There were strange carvings on the walls. Fake torches gave off a soft, dancing light. Cold fog covered the floor.

There was no sign of the hand-creature.

CLACK! Something moved at the far end of the room. Alexander crept toward the noise. The floor felt ice-cold through his footie pajamas.

He came to a tall, golden box. There were snakes and beetles carved on the sides. A skull was painted on top.

The mummy case! he thought.

The torches flickered. The case started to shake. Then the lid popped open!

"AUGHGHH!" Alexander jumped back.

"*EEP!* Don't hurt me!" screamed the pale, ghostly figure inside.

Alexander stopped. He blinked a few times. "Mr. Hoarsely? What are you doing in there?"

Mr. Hoarsely was shaking like a jackhammer. "That guard spooked me. I ran down here and guess what?! The mummy case was wide open, and *empty*! So I hid inside!" he said. "The Bumpy Mummy must be *alive*!"

"I *knew* I saw it yesterday," said Alexander.

"Y-y-you did?" said Mr. Hoarsely.

"Yes. But wait," said Alexander. "I thought the mummy only came alive if someone stole the Ruby Scorpion. And I just saw the scorpion upstairs. It's safe and protected by lasers!"

"Lasers-shmasers!!" Mr. Hoarsely shouted. "The mummy is definitely out *there* because it's not in *here*! Case closed!"

SLAM! Mr. Hoarsely shut the mummy case.

Alexander thought about what Mr. Hoarsely had said. He zipped to the exit, cutting through the swirling fog.

CHAPTER 11
DON'T LET YOUR GUARD DOWN

Alexander sprinted up the steps and into the lobby. His dad and Mr. Plunkett were laying out the sleeping bags. Rip and Nikki saw Alexander. They ran over.

"Salamander!" said Nikki. "Where did you go?"

"You totally missed the gift shop!" said Rip, holding a toy gopher. "Check it out! A Stermont Stella bobblehead!"

Alexander grabbed his friends' shoulders.

"Guys," he said, "I don't care about the gift shop! Listen to me: I was right! The Bumpy Mummy *is* alive!!"

Rip and Nikki looked at each other.

"The mummy is not in its case! Mr. Hoarsely is down there right now," said Alexander. "Ask him!"

Rip, Nikki, and the bobblehead nodded.

"IT'S BUMPY-MUMMY TIME, STUDENTS!" shouted Mr. Plunkett. "Gather around to hear about Stermont's most famous mummy! Then we'll head downstairs to the mummy's chamber."

Alexander, Rip, and Nikki joined the rest of their class.

"Some people say the Bumpy Mummy was an old circus dummy created to sell tickets," said Mr. Plunkett. "Others say it was a nearsighted cowboy who sat on a cactus, and had to be covered in bandages. Or even worse: a wart-covered toad-person!"

Alexander's dad munched a handful of popcorn. "So scary," he whispered.

"And," continued Mr. Plunkett, "the Bumpy Mummy will come back to life if —"

"The Ruby Scorpion has been stolen!"

Everyone gasped.

Ms. Sargent stomped into the lobby, swinging her flashlight.

“Someone got past my lasers!” said the guard. She shined her light in Mr. Plunkett’s eyes. “I’ve been working here for years with *zero* funny business. But on the night *your* class arrives, our greatest treasure goes missing!?”

Ms. Sargent swept her light across the students’ faces. “You *toddlers* stay put while I search the museum. If so much as *one toe* leaves a sleeping bag, I’ll lock you up!”

Her footsteps echoed across the stone floor as she marched away.

“Whoa,” whispered Nikki. “She’s so —”

“Awesome!” said Rip.

Alexander grabbed Rip’s elbow. “Look!” He pointed up to the balcony.

A grayish-white figure, covered in strange little bumps, stood at the railing. It was staring at Alexander.

CHAPTER 12 TICKTOCK

The mummy locked eyes with Alexander. Then it turned and ran.

"It's running!" said Alexander. "I bet it's got the ruby!"

"Follow that mummy!" whispered Nikki.

"Are you nuts?" said Rip. "Ms. Sargent is super tough! Let *her* catch the thief."

"She can stop regular thieves, but only *we* can stop monster thieves! We're the S.S.M.P.," said Alexander.

"Okay, okay," said Rip. "Hooray for us and stuff."

"We'll need to be extra-sneaky," said Nikki. "If that guard sees us, she'll lock us up!"

"Come on!" said Alexander. He hurried to the balcony steps.

Rip and Nikki followed.

"Pj's are great for sneaking around," whispered Nikki. "My slippers are ninja-quiet!"

They crept up to the second floor.

"No sign of the mummy," said Nikki.

"It must be hiding," said Alexander. "Keep looking!"

They searched a suit of armor, a wigwam, a triceratops skeleton, a fake volcano, and even a stagecoach.

"The mummy must've gotten away," said Rip.

"But how?!" asked Alexander. "We were —"

"*Shhh!*" said Nikki. "Someone's coming!"

A beam of light danced through the darkness, throwing long shadows across the floor.

"STAY WHERE YOU ARE, THIEF!" shouted a voice. "AND NO FUNNY BUSINESS!"

"It's Ms. Sargent!" whispered Alexander. "Run!"

They scrambled to keep out of the light. The three friends ducked down near an odd wooden door shaped like an acorn.

"Let's hide in there," said Nikki. She pushed on the door. It wouldn't budge.

"I've got this," said Rip. He rolled up his sleeves and leaned into the door. *"Grugghhh,"* he grunted. "It's stuck! And it's making a weird noise."

TICKTOCK, TICKTOCK, TICKTOCK!

"I know that sound!" said Alexander. "Rip! Nikki! Duck!"

"Huh?" said Rip.

"It's not a duck!" said Nikki. "It's a cuckoo!" She jerked Rip away from the door.

BONGGGG!!!

A spine-shaking chime rang out like a thunderclap.

The acorn door popped open. And a giant mechanical bird sprung out!

"Grab that cuckoo!" Alexander said. The three of them hugged the cuckoo. It wobbled a bit, and then yanked them through the doorway.

A second later, Ms. Sargent's light flashed across the closed acorn door.

Alexander, Nikki, and Rip tumbled into a dark room. They could hear loud gears whirring all around them.

"Where are we?" asked Alexander.

"Nikki, use your see-in-the-dark powers!" said Rip.

"Uh, we are inside the world's second-largest cuckoo clock," she whispered. "And we're not alone."

CHAPTER 13

HICKORY DICKORY BOPP

Alexander's eyes slowly adjusted to the pale green light inside the clock. He saw gears, cogs, chains, and levers everywhere. And right in front of his nose, the Bumpy Mummy.

"Ack!" Alexander jumped back. But the mummy just stood there. Or rather, leaned there.

"The mummy's not moving," said Nikki. She stepped up and poked its chest. A cloud of dust poofed up.

"It's so old and dirty!" said Alexander. "But the mummy we saw looked shiny and clean!"

"And alive," said Rip. "This one's just leaning against that old cart."

Alexander stepped closer to the cart. It was piled high with junk. A glint of gold caught his eye. "Hey!" he said. "My dad's mirror!"

"And my skates!" said Nikki.

"And my mom's trumpet!" said Rip. "And there's Hoarsely's dustpan! All of the stolen stuff is here!"

Alexander reached out for the Reflecto-900, but stopped. It had been taped to the cart. He looked at the other objects. They were all stuck to the cart.

"This cart looks like a machine," he said. "A machine made from shiny stuff. But what's it do?"

KRICKLE-KRICKLE!

"IT HELPS ME STEAL THE SHINIEST TREASURE EVER!" shouted a squeaky voice from high in the clockworks.

A lumpy figure swung down on a chain.

"*That's* the mummy we saw on the balcony!" said Nikki.

"And look! It's missing a hand!" yelled Alexander.

This bigger, scarier, *moving* mummy didn't walk stiffly like a mummy from an old movie. It glided along, making crinkly noises with each step.

KRICKLE-KRICKLE!

"It sounds like that mummy's wearing a diaper," said Rip.

POP-POP!

The mummy's face twisted into an angry scowl. "WHAT?! I am *not* wearing a diaper!" it said. "And I'm not *really* a mummy!"

The monster drifted into the light. It was wrapped in some kind of shiny material, covered with little plastic circles.

"A bubble-wrap monster!?!" said Alexander.

"I'm a bubble-wrap WARRIOR!" boomed the monster. "And I am ready to rumble!"

CHAPTER 14 BUBBLE TROUBLE

Alexander, Rip, and Nikki backed away from the crinkling, snapping, one-handed bubble-wrap warrior.

Alexander shouted over the grinding clock gears. "So *you* sent us the striped boxes and stole our stuff!?"

"Yes!" said the bubble-wrap warrior. "You humans are so annoying! You use bubble wrap to protect your shiny treasures. But then, when you no longer need us, you pop us! That hurts, you know?! I did it all for payback!"

The monster's voice grew louder as it bounced closer to the three friends.

"Instead of protecting your shiniest treasures, I *stole* them!" said the bubble-wrap warrior. "First I mailed my little helping hands to every house in town —"

"The bubble wrap *inside* the striped boxes!" said Nikki.

"Exactly," said the monster. "But things like skates and trumpets weren't valuable enough. I needed *bigger, shinier* treasure! Then I heard your teacher talking about the Ruby Scorpion. So I built an awesome laser-bouncing machine from your junk!"

"But why are you pretending to be the Bumpy Mummy?" asked Rip.

"To blend in!" said the bubble-wrap warrior. "It's easy to hide in a museum when you look like a mummy! I kept lookout while my helping hand popped off to steal this — *Stermont's greatest treasure!* "

The bubble-wrap warrior raised its handless arm toward the shadows above.

Just then, the bubble-wrap hand dropped down from the gears. It was clutching the Ruby Scorpion!

It scampered up the bubble-wrap warrior's leg, and snapped itself to the end of the monster's arm.

"At last, I am complete!" said the warrior. "Now that I have the ruby, there's just one thing left for me to *wrap* up."

The monster puffed itself up.

Then it lunged at Alexander.

CHAPTER 15

A TIGHT SQUEEZE

"Oof!" The bubble-wrap warrior barreled into Alexander, trapping him in a bear hug.

Rip and Nikki pulled at the monster. It laughed. "Let's go for a spin, shall we? I think my true form will BLOW YOU AWAY!"

The bubble-wrap warrior tossed Alexander aside. It set the Ruby Scorpion down on a big wooden pinecone.

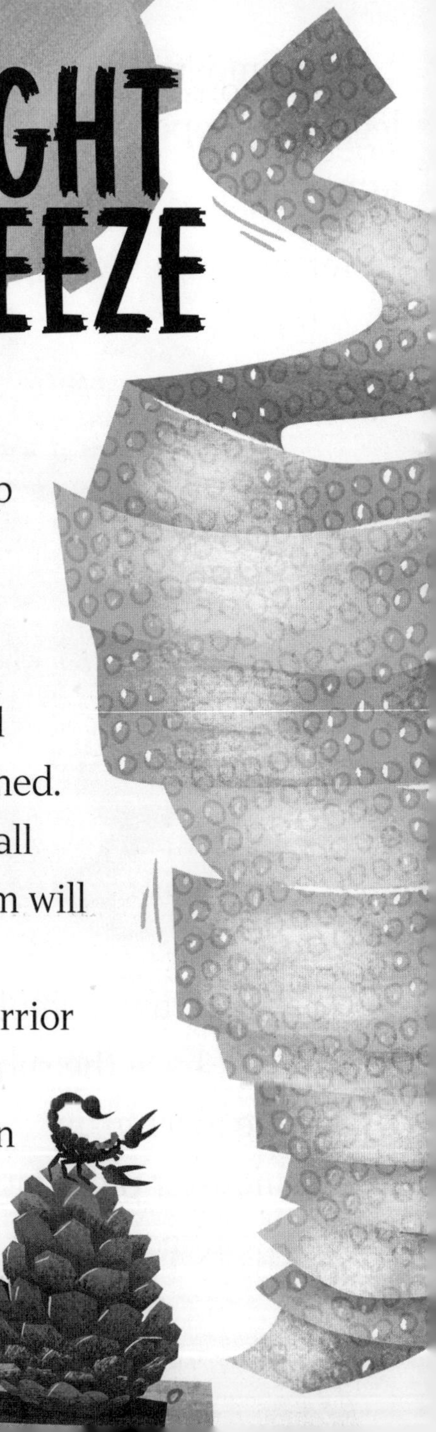

The monster unraveled itself into one long noodle made of hundreds of sheets of bubble wrap. Then it began spinning around. It spun faster and faster, rising in the air like a giant tornado. A giant twisting, snapping tornado made entirely of bubble wrap!

WHOOOOOOSH! The three friends' hair started blowing.

Nikki shouted something. But Alexander couldn't hear her over the rush of wind.

The bubble-wrap warrior spun even faster. Clock gears wobbled. Chains rattled. Alexander could barely stand against the strong wind. He saw Nikki clinging to a ladder. Rip crouched behind a cog.

Alexander grabbed the closest thing — the tail feathers of the giant cuckoo. He held on tight.

FLOMP! Eight long arms shot out of the tornado.

"Watch out! This monster's going into octopus-mode!" Rip shouted.

A bubbly arm stretched across the room and grabbed Rip.

"Gotcha!" said the bubble-wrap warrior.

Another arm reached for Nikki. She scooted up the ladder and out of reach.

A third arm snaked back to Alexander, wrapping around his leg. He hugged the cuckoo tighter. Then two more arms shot out and — **SNAP!** — broke the wooden bird off its branch.

"AAACK!" yelled Alexander.

The monster grinned as it grabbed Rip and Alexander. "Let's see how *you* guys like getting popped!"

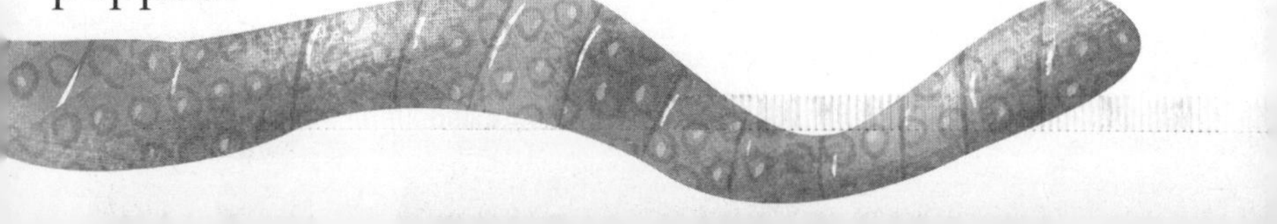

CHAPTER 16

POP 'TIL YOU DROP

The bubble-wrap warrior squeezed Rip and Alexander until their eyes bulged.

"Drop my friends, bubble brain!" yelled Nikki.

She sat on a platform near the clock's face, dangling her legs over the edge. She stuck out her arm, jiggling something red and shiny over the grinding gears.

"The Ruby Scorpion!" said Alexander.

"Warrior, if you don't put my friends down," she said, "I'll toss *this* into the gears!"

"You wouldn't dare ruin Stermont's shiniest treasure!" growled the monster. It squeezed the boys tighter.

"Sure I would!" said Nikki. She tossed the red shiny scorpion into the clock's gears.

CRRUNNNCHH!!!

Shiny red pebbles tinkled down through the gears.

"NOOOO!!!!" the bubble-wrap warrior screamed. The monster dropped the boys and reached for the gears.

POP-POP! One of its arms got twisted in a cog.

Alexander rolled to his feet. He was standing near the broken cuckoo.

"SQUAAAAARRK!" The monster let out an angry battle squeak. It raised its puffy fists high, ready to smash.

"Guys, quick!" Alexander shouted. "Over here!"

Rip and Nikki ran over.

Together, the three friends lifted the cuckoo. Then they pointed it at the monster's head.

"Hey, bubbles!" said Alexander. "Watch the birdie!"

He pulled a latch near the cuckoo's spring.

BOING!

The bird delivered a cuckoo punch, right on the monster's nose. The monster fell backward. The rest of its long arms became tangled in the clockwork gears.

It sounded like the Fourth of July as the bubble-wrap warrior was pressed between the gears, building up to one final clock-rocking **BOOM!**

"Nikki, I can't believe you destroyed the Ruby Scorpion!" said Alexander.

"What?! No way!" said Nikki. "That was a paperweight I bought in the gift shop." She pulled the real Ruby Scorpion from her pocket.

CLICK-CLICK-CLICK-WHIRR!

The clock's gears spat out a flat, clear sheet of plastic.

"Looks like every last bubble's been popped," said Nikki.

"So, what now?" asked Rip. "Ms. Sargent will lock us up if she sees us with the Ruby Scorpion!"

"Hmmm," said Alexander. "Let's prop the clock door open and leave it here for her to find."

"Along with all the other missing stuff!" said Nikki.

The friends snuck out of the clock. They went down to the basement to tell Mr. Hoarsely the coast was clear. Then they crept up to the lobby and climbed into their sleeping bags.

"Toddlers, wake up!" Ms. Sargent came running into the lobby. "I found the Ruby Scorpion! And a bunch of other junk."

Ms. Sargent dumped the stolen items on the floor. The students and Mr. Plunkett cheered. They jumped up to grab their missing skates, trumpets, and shiny doodads.

"Dad!" said Alexander. "Look!" He handed his dad the Reflecto-900.

"Woo-hoo!" cried his dad. Then he leaped up and did another front-porch dance.

"Ha-ha!" said Nikki. "What a great field trip!"

"You mean, what a great first day of summer vacation!" said Rip.

Alexander gave Rip and Nikki a high thirty. (Two high fifteens in a row.) Then, by the glow of the world's second-largest cuckoo clock, he added another monster to the notebook.

BUBBLE-WRAP WARRIOR

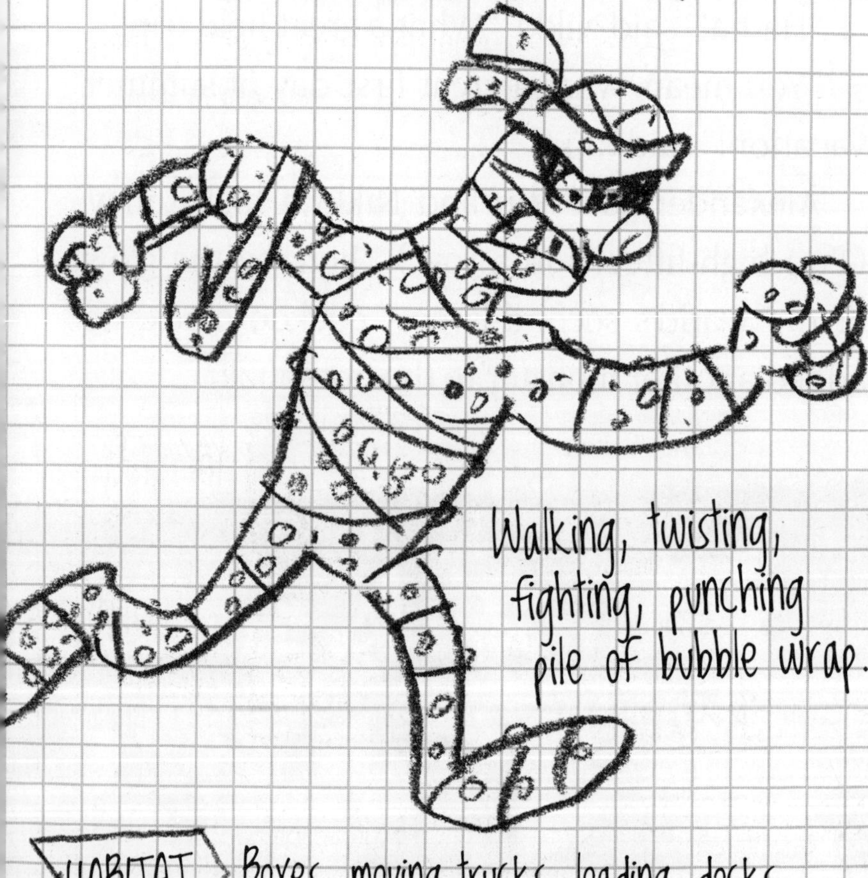

Walking, twisting, fighting, punching pile of bubble wrap.

HABITAT Boxes, moving trucks, loading docks.

PIP-PIP-POP! A bubble-wrap warrior would lose in a fight with a forkupine.

BEHAVIOR

Bubble-wrap warriors like to steal treasure.

FUN FACT!

These monsters are clever. They can turn a pile of shiny junk into a laser-blocking machine!

BEWARE!

Bubble-wrap warriors can twist themselves into many shapes:

mummy

tornado

octopus

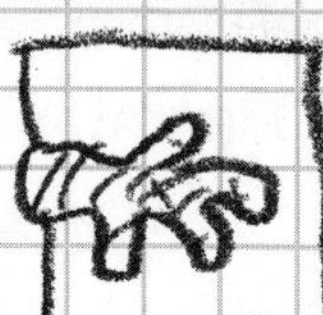

crawling hand

WARNING!

If you find a sheet of bubble wrap, pop EVERY BUBBLE! Just to be safe.

TROY CUMMINGS

has no tail, no wings, no fangs, no claws, and only one head. As a kid, he believed that monsters might really exist. Today, he's sure of it.

BEHAVIOR When this creature is not writing or drawing, he is cleaning out the cat box.

HABITAT A creaky chair in front of the computer screen.

DIET Lemon custard.

(NOTE: Troy washes his hands before eating. You know, because of the cat box and all.)

EVIDENCE Few people believe that Troy Cummings is real. The only proof we have is that he supposedly wrote and illustrated The Eensy-Weensy Spider Freaks Out!, and Giddy-up, Daddy!

WARNING Keep your eyes peeled for more danger in The Notebook of Doom #7:

FLURRY OF THE SNOMBIES